THIS BOOK BELONGS TO:

_____

Dedicated to all the explorers.

All rights reserved.
No part of this book may be reproduced in any form or by any means, electronic or mechanical, and no photocopying or recording, unless you have written permission from the author.

ISBN 978-1-958985-74-8

Text copyright © 2025 by Mimi Jones

www.joeysavestheday.com

A Mimi Book

Washington is the only state named in honor of a U.S. president. George Washington was the very first leader of the country. His name reminds us of courage, leadership, and new beginnings.

Washington was the forty-second state to join the Union. It officially joined on November 11, 1889.

Washington is located in the Northwest region of the United States and is bordered by two states: Idaho and Oregon.

Olympia is the capital of Washington.
It officially became the capital in 1853.

Olympia, Washington, has an estimated population of about 56,270 people.

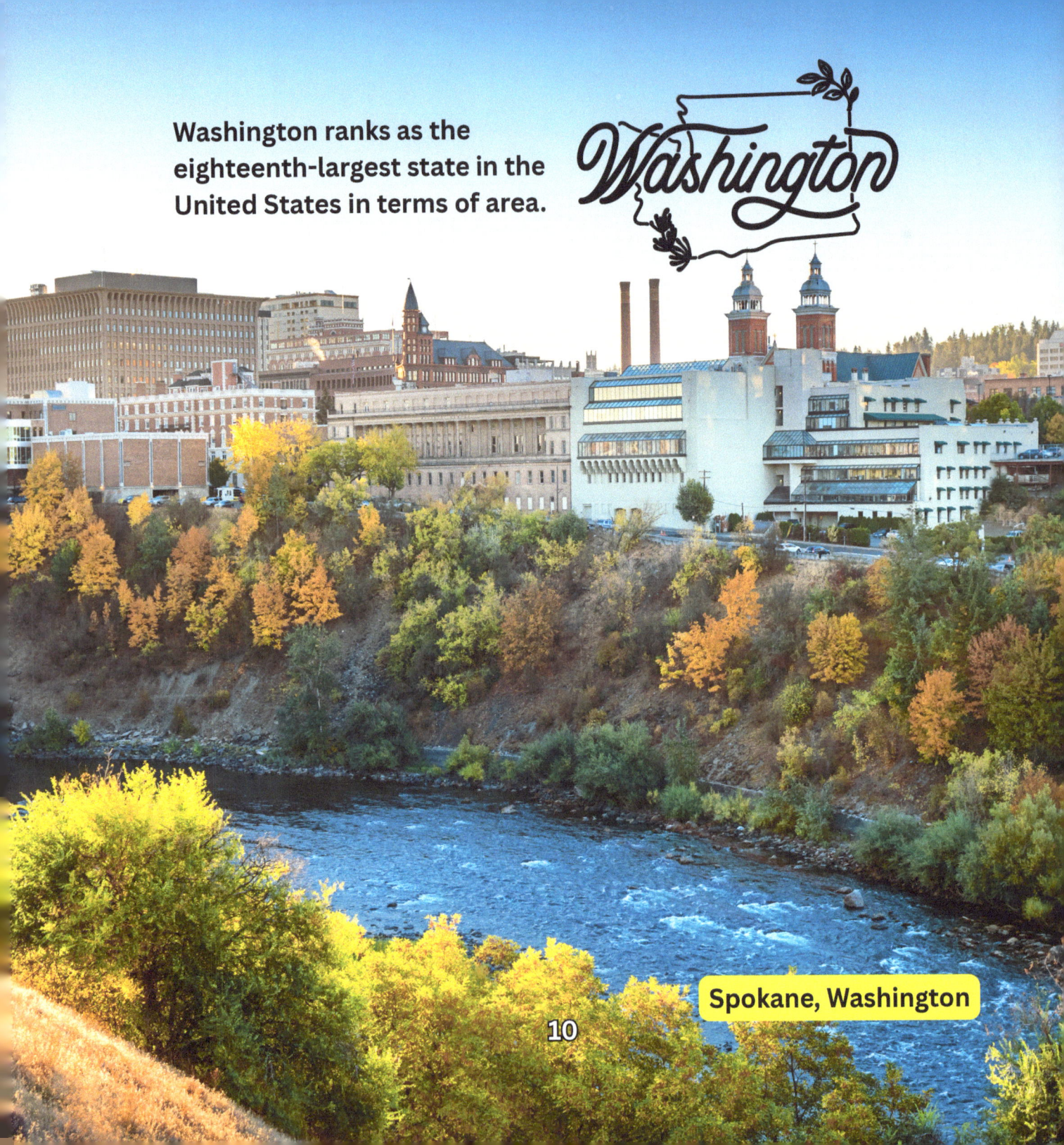

Washington ranks as the eighteenth-largest state in the United States in terms of area.

Spokane, Washington

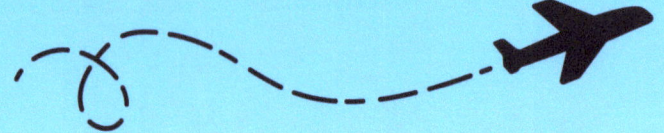

Although William Boeing was born in Detroit, Michigan, in 1881, he later relocated to Seattle, Washington, and had a significant impact. He founded the Boeing Company, which built airplanes that enabled people to travel faster and farther than ever before. His inventions took flight right from Washington, and today, the skies are still filled with the ideas he helped launch.

The Space Needle was built in Seattle for the 1962 World's Fair. It was designed to showcase futuristic ideas, and it certainly looked the part! With its tall legs and round top, many people thought it resembled a flying saucer, ready to take off. Today, it's one of the most famous landmarks in Washington State.

WASHINGTON

There are 39 counties in Washington.

Here is a list of twenty of those counties:

Adams	Douglas	Klickitat	Stevens
Benton	Ferry	Lincoln	Thurston
Clallam	Garfield	Pacific	Walla Walla
Columbia	Island	Pierce	Whitman
Cowlitz	King	Spokane	Yakima

PARK

Deception Pass State Park is a scenic park in northwest Washington, known for its tall bridge, forest trails, and swirling ocean waters. It's located on Whidbey Island and Fidalgo Island, about 90 minutes north of Seattle.

Cattle Point Light stands at the southern tip of San Juan Island, Washington. Built in 1935, this small lighthouse replaced an earlier lantern that guided ships through foggy waters. The area got its name from the Hudson's Bay Company, which once unloaded cattle nearby.

The La Conner Rainbow Bridge, located in La Conner, Washington, is a striking red arch bridge that crosses the Swinomish Channel. Completed in 1957, this bridge serves as a vital connection between the mainland and Fidalgo Island.

Olympic National Park is in Washington State, where mountains, rainforests, and beaches all come together. You can hike through mossy woods, splash in tide pools, or spot elk in snowy meadows.

LET'S GO HIKING

The Washington state bird is the American Goldfinch. It was chosen as the state bird in 1951.

The official Washington state flower is the Pacific Coast rhododendron. It was chosen as the state flower in 1959.

Washington's nicknames are the Evergreen State and the Green Tree State.

-the-  STATE

-the-

  STATE

The Washington state motto, "Alki" or "Al-ki," is derived from the Native American language of the local tribes and translates to "By and By."

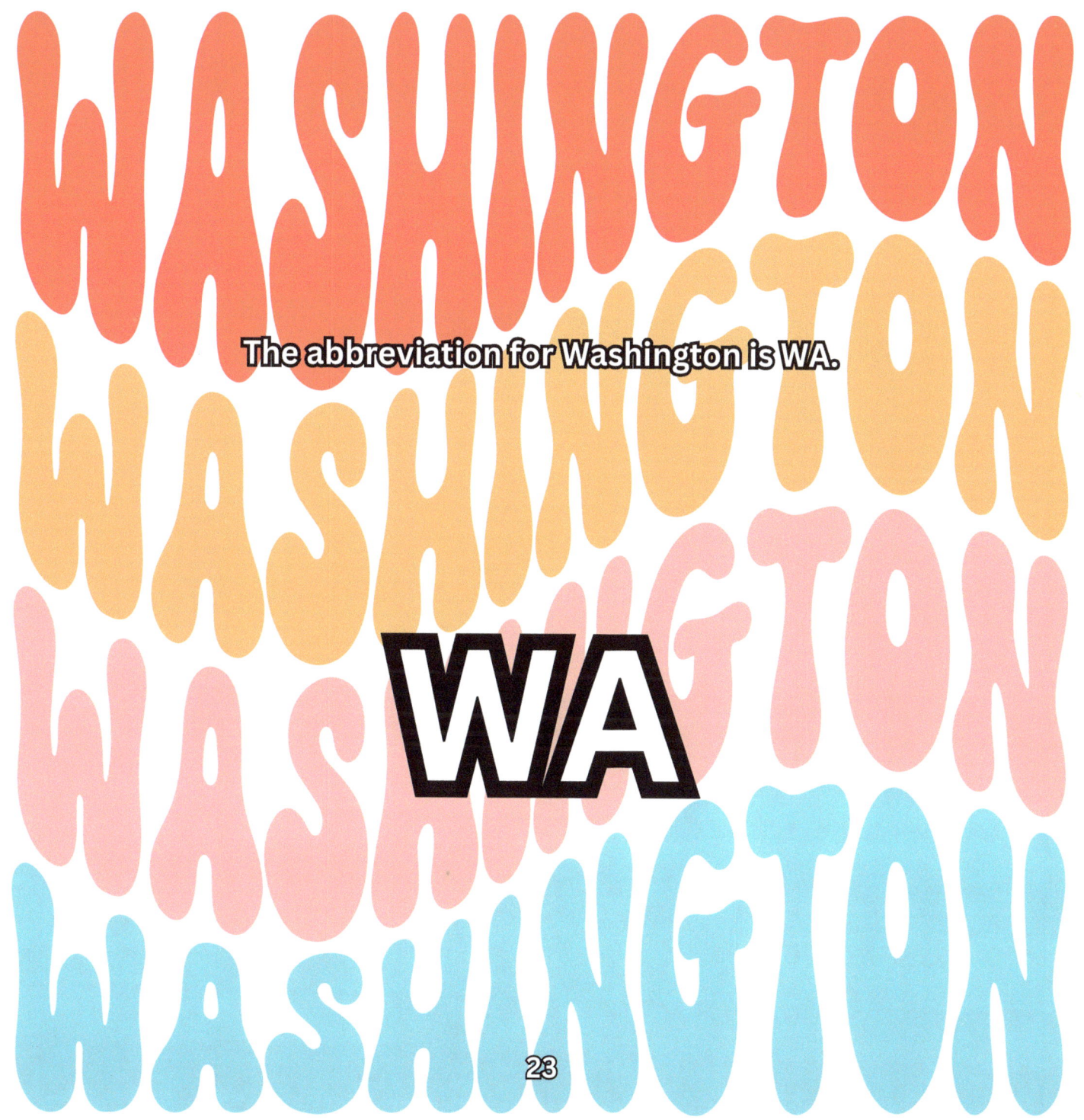

The abbreviation for Washington is WA.

Washington's state flag was officially adopted on March 5, 1923.

Some crops grown in Washington are apples, asparagus, blueberries, legumes, peas, potatoes, and wheat.

Some animals that live in Washington are black bears, coyotes, elk, raccoons, and snowshoe hares.

Washington experiences significant temperature variations throughout the year. The highest temperature ever recorded in the state was 120 degrees Fahrenheit, reached in Hanford on June 29, 2021. Conversely, the lowest temperature recorded was -48 degrees Fahrenheit, noted in Mazama on December 30, 1968.

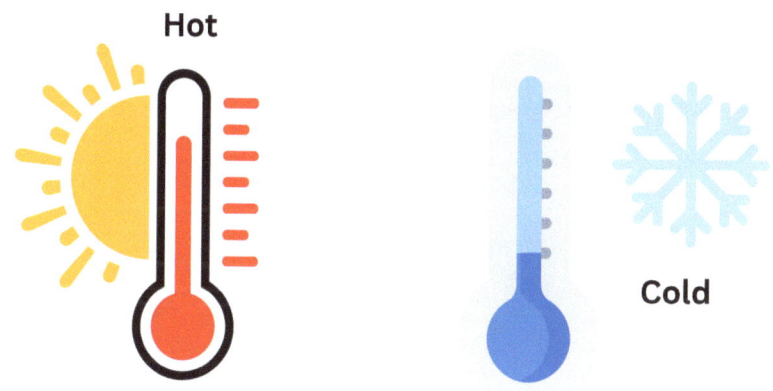

Seattle, Washington

The Seattle Great Wheel is a giant Ferris wheel located on Pier 57 along Seattle's waterfront. It stands 175 feet tall and offers enclosed gondola rides with stunning views of Elliott Bay and the city skyline.

Washington State Ferries is the largest ferry system in the United States, and it's based in Puget Sound, connecting cities and islands across the region. The ferries travel between places like Seattle, Bainbridge Island, Whidbey Island, Kingston, and Bremerton.

Bellingham International Airport is a friendly gateway to the skies, located just three miles northwest of the city of Bellingham in Whatcom County, Washington. Nestled near the Canadian border, this airport is a popular choice for travelers from both the United States and Canada.

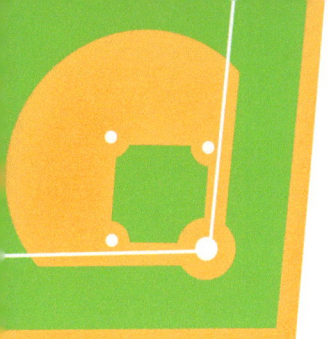

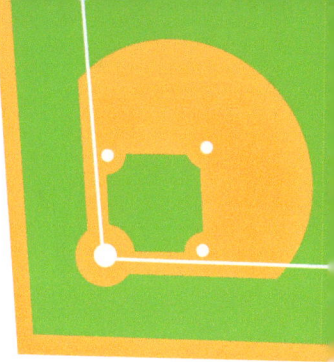

The Seattle Mariners are Washington's Major League Baseball team. They play at T-Mobile Park in Seattle and wear navy blue and teal. Founded in 1977, the team is known for exciting games and legendary players like Ken Griffey Jr.

FOOTBALL

The Seattle Seahawks are a professional football team based in Seattle, Washington. They play in the NFL and host games at Lumen Field, where fans are famously loud and proud—earning the nickname "12s." The team won its first Super Bowl in 2014 and wears colors inspired by the Pacific Northwest: blue, green, and silver.

Washington

Washington's state tree is the Western Hemlock, chosen in 1947. It's a tall evergreen with soft, feathery needles and a droopy top that looks like it's bowing. These trees love cool, rainy forests and can live for hundreds of years. The Western Hemlock reminds us of quiet strength and natural beauty in the Pacific Northwest.

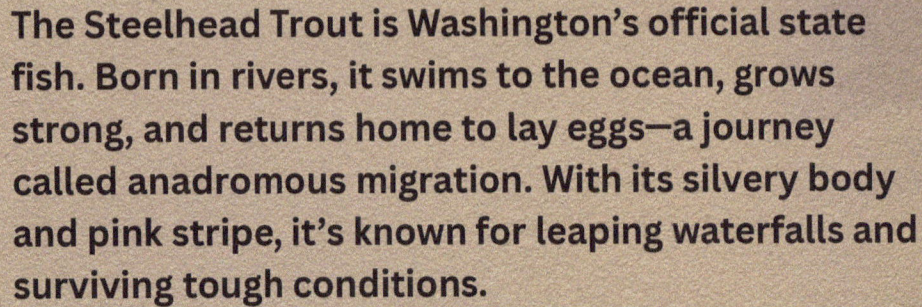

The Steelhead Trout is Washington's official state fish. Born in rivers, it swims to the ocean, grows strong, and returns home to lay eggs—a journey called anadromous migration. With its silvery body and pink stripe, it's known for leaping waterfalls and surviving tough conditions.

WASHINGTON

Can you name these?

I hope you enjoyed learning about Washington.

To explore fun facts about the other 49 states, visit my website at www.joeysavestheday.com. You'll also find a wide variety of homeschool resources to support joyful learning at home. If you enjoyed this book, I would be grateful if you left a review. Your feedback truly helps. Thank you for your support!

Check out these other interesting books in the 50 States Fact Books Series!

www.mimibooks.com

www.ingramcontent.com/pod-product-compliance
Lightning Source LLC
Chambersburg PA
CBHW040028050426
42453CB00002B/45